Made in the USA
Monee, IL
10 June 2023

35556636R00057